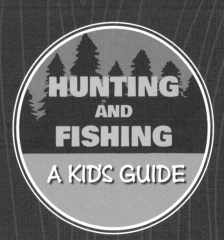

HUNTING
AND
FISHING

A KID'S GUIDE

We're Going
SMALL-GAME
HUNTING

Kaylee Gilmore

PowerKiDS press.

New York

D1060653

Published in 2017 by The Rosen Publishing Group, Inc.
29 East 21st Street, New York, NY 10010

Copyright © 2017 by The Rosen Publishing Group, Inc.

All rights reserved. No part of this book may be reproduced in any form without permission in writing from the publisher, except by a reviewer.

First Edition

Editor: Melissa Raé Shofner
Book Design: Tanya Dellaccio

Photo Credits: Cover FotoRequest/Shutterstock.com; back cover, pp. 1, 3–4, 6–8, 10–12, 14, 16, 18–22, 24, 26, 28, 30–32 (background) ArtBitz/Shutterstock.com; all pages except p. 2 (wood texture) sittipong/Shutterstock.com; p. 4 Sharon Day/Shutterstock.com; p. 5 BMJ/Shutterstock.com; p. 6 John E Heintz Jr/Shutterstock.com; p. 7 (badger) charlie davidson/Shutterstock.com; p. 7 (weasel) Erni/Shutterstock.com; p. 7 (porcupine) A_Lein/Shutterstock.com; p. 7 (armadillo) IrinaK/Shutterstock.com; p. 9 Lisa Hagan/Shutterstock.com; p. 11 (raccoon tracks) Jarrod Erbe/Shutterstock.com; p. 11 (raccoon) andamanec/Shutterstock.com; p. 13 Craig Moore/Getty Images; p. 14 Nikitin Victor/Shutterstock.com; p. 15 Steve Oehlenschlager/Shutterstock.com; p. 17 Volt Collection/Shutterstock.com; p. 19 (dachshund) eans/Shutterstock.com; p. 19 (beagle) dezi/Shutterstock.com; p. 19 (coonhound) SubertT/Shutterstock.com; pp. 21 (hunter), 30 studio0411/Shutterstock.com; p. 21 (squirrel) Pi-Lens/Shutterstock.com; p. 22 Paul Reeves Photography/Shutterstock.com; p. 23 J Bespoy Photography/Getty Images; p. 25 Scenic Shutterbug/Shutterstock.com; p. 26 Howard Sandler/Shutterstock.com; p. 27 Yuval Helfman/Shutterstock.com; p. 29 Carl Day/Shutterstock.com.

Cataloging-in-Publication Data

Names: Gilmore, Kaylee.
Title: We're going small-game hunting / Kaylee Gilmore.
Description: New York : PowerKids Press, 2017. | Series: Hunting and fishing: a kid's guide | Includes index.
Identifiers: ISBN 9781499427479 (pbk.) | ISBN 9781499428711 (library bound) | ISBN 9781508152835 (6 pack)
Subjects: LCSH: Small game hunting–Juvenile literature.
Classification: LCC SK340.G55 2017 | DDC 799.2'5–dc23

Manufactured in the United States of America

CPSIA Compliance Information: Batch Batch #BW17PK: For Further Information contact Rosen Publishing, New York, New York at 1-800-237-9932

CONTENTS

A NOTE TO READERS
Always talk with a parent or teacher before proceeding with any of the activities found in this book. Some activities require adult supervision.

A NOTE TO PARENTS AND TEACHERS
This book was written to be informative and entertaining. Some of the activities in this book require adult supervision. Please talk with your child or student before allowing them to proceed with any hunting activities. The author and publisher specifically disclaim any liability for injury or damages that may result from use of information in this book.

A HARDER HUNT

Some people think that small animals are easier to hunt than large animals. This isn't always true. Small-game hunting presents many **challenges**. For example, small animals can use their size to their advantage. After all, the smaller the animal, the smaller the **target**! It's also easier for small creatures to find places to hide. Have you ever tried to find a scared animal that didn't want to be seen? It's hard, unless you know where and how to look.

HUNTING HINT

Squirrels have sharp claws that are great for climbing. Their bushy tails help them balance on branches. It's hard to spot squirrels hiding in trees.

4

It's easy for small animals to hide. The more you hunt, the better you'll be at spotting them.

WHAT IS SMALL GAME?

If you're going hunting, it's important to know what animals are considered small game. You should check the website of your state's wildlife department to find out what small-game animals can be hunted in your area. Your state might consider some birds to be small game. Be sure to check the rules, though, since hunting birds is entirely different from hunting other animals. In this book, we will talk about hunting small animals such as squirrels, rabbits, foxes, and raccoons.

HUNTING HINT

Some small-game animals have more than one name. For example, groundhogs are also called woodchucks and marmots.

These are some small-game animals that can be hunted in the United States.

weasel

badger

armadillo

porcupine

WHEN TO HUNT

An animal's "season" is the time period when it can be hunted. It can be hard to keep all of the small-game seasons straight because there are so many.

Some animals are always in season, but make sure you know your state's laws before you go hunting. Imagine you're hunting squirrels, and you have a perfect shot at a rabbit. Don't shoot unless you're sure rabbit is in season. It's against the law to hunt animals that aren't in season.

HUNTING HINT

Some small-game animals are nocturnal, which means they sleep during the day and are awake at night. You'll have a better chance of finding the type of animal you're hunting if you know when it's most active.

In Michigan, opossums are always in season. They can be hunted all year, and there are no limits on how many one hunter can shoot.

WHERE TO HUNT

Small-game animals can be found in many places, including forests and fields. If you can, visit an area before hunting there. Walk around, keeping an eye out for signs of small game, such as animal trails and droppings.

There are also special areas called state game lands that are owned by the government. You're welcome to hunt on these lands, but be careful. Hikers and dog walkers also use these areas. Don't take a shot unless you're sure of your target.

HUNTING HINT

Always make sure you know who owns the land you're hunting on. Don't forget to double-check that you're allowed to hunt there.

Before setting off on a hunt, it's a good idea to learn to recognize the tracks of the animals that live in the area. These are raccoon tracks.

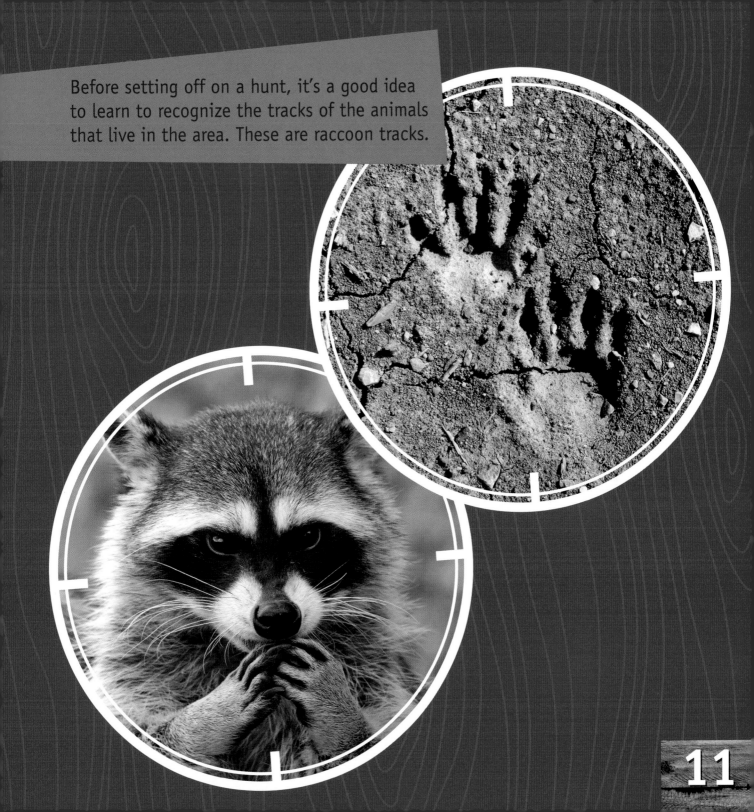

RULES OF THE SPORT

Before going hunting, you'll need to pass a course that teaches you how to safely hunt using firearms, or guns. If you pass the test at the end of the course, you'll be able to purchase a hunting **license** from your state. Depending on your age and where you live, you may need a licensed adult to hunt with you.

Most states allow you to shoot several animals in a single day. The "bag limit" is the top number of animals you're allowed to kill. Hunters who go over this number are breaking the law.

HUNTING HINT

It's a good idea to buy a warm jacket to wear when hunting. Many hunting jackets have pockets that are deep enough to carry small kills.

Hunters wear bright "blaze" orange so that other hunters can easily see them.

13

CHOOSING A FIREARM

Many small-game hunters believe shotguns are the best firearms for hunting small game. Shotguns scatter dozens of **pellets**, called shot, over a short range. This means you must get closer to your target, but you have a much better chance of hitting it.

A rifle is a long gun that's held against the shoulder when fired. Rifles shoot single **bullets** that cause lots of damage, or harm. It can be harder to use a rifle to shoot a small, fast animal.

.22 rifle

HUNTING HINT

Small rifles are often used when hunting **vermin**, such as groundhogs. Vermin hunters use .22 rifles that use small bullets and make little noise when fired.

This young hunter is practicing his shot to become a better hunter. It's important to practice before going out on a hunt.

BOWHUNTING

Small-game hunters who are looking for a greater challenge might want to try bowhunting. It's very hard to hit a small animal with an arrow. Arrows are slower than shot or bullets. The animal has more time to move after the arrow is let go.

Most hunters use a compound bow. This type of bow uses cables and **pulleys** that make it easier to pull back an arrow. Successful small-game bowhunters have great aim and lots of luck.

HUNTING HINT

Many states require you to take a bowhunting safety course. You'll also need to get a hunting license.

Bowhunting is hard because you need to get closer to your target than if you were hunting with a gun.

MAN'S BEST FRIEND

Small-game animals can be hard to find when out on a hunt. Some hunters like to use dogs to help them. A good hunting dog has a powerful sense of smell and excellent hunting **instincts**, and it doesn't shy away from the sound of gunshots.

Certain dogs are easily trained to be excellent hunters. Coonhounds are great at hunting raccoons. Beagles are very good rabbit and hare hunters. Hunting with beagles is so popular that it is often called beagling. All types of hounds make great hunting helpers.

HUNTING HINT

It's a good idea for your hunting dog to wear some blaze orange, too. This will help you and other hunters know where it is.

Today, dachshunds are used to hunt small game such as groundhogs and rabbits. They were first used to hunt badgers.

dachshund

coonhound

beagle

SPEEDY SQUIRRELS

Squirrels love to hide in trees. They're hard to spot because of colors and patterns in their coat that help them blend in with their surroundings. This is called camouflage.

Squirrel hunters often use a method called still-hunting. This might sound as though you sit down in one spot and wait, but there's more to still-hunting than that. Still-hunters move slowly and silently. They stop often to look and listen. Like many other animals, squirrels are good at seeing movement. Sometimes, though, still-hunters can catch them by surprise.

American red squirrels are very fast and are great jumpers and climbers. In summer, a black stripe appears on their sides.

HUNTING HINT

Keep your eyes and ears open when you're hunting. If you're not having much luck finding small game, try moving to a different area.

Sometimes a hunter will corner a squirrel up a tree. If the hunter walks around the tree, the squirrel will move to the opposite side of the tree. How can you get the squirrel into view?

If you're hunting with two or more people, one hunter can stand absolutely still while another hunter walks around the tree. The squirrel will circle until the first hunter has a shot. If you're hunting on your own, try throwing something small at the tree, such as a stone or a branch.

HUNTING HINT

Make sure you know where the other hunters are when hunting in a group. You'll learn how to hunt safely in a group when you take a hunting safety course.

Eastern gray squirrels can also have black fur. Both colors are common in much of the United States.

RACCOONS UP A TREE

Raccoons are often hunted for their soft, thick fur. Since they're nocturnal, it's better to hunt them at night. Raccoon hunting is easier with the help of dogs. Hounds can smell raccoons and corner them in trees.

Trapping an animal in a tree is called treeing. Unlike a treed squirrel, a treed raccoon can be easily shot. Treeing is where the phrase "barking up the wrong tree" comes from. If a hound is barking up the wrong tree, it's not a very good hunting dog.

HUNTING HINT

Whether it's day or night, never shoot until you are absolutely sure of your target.

Raccoons like hiding in tree branches the best. Sometimes they'll also hide in woodpiles, hollow trees, or holes in the ground.

RABBITS ON THE RUN

Rabbits are hard to find because they like to hide in heavy brush. They have great camouflage. You have to get them to show themselves before you can successfully hunt them.

One method for hunting rabbits is to startle, or scare, them out of their hiding places and into the open. You can do this by kicking and stamping in thick brush. If there is snow on the ground, tracking rabbits is easy. Following a rabbit's footprints will often lead you to its location.

HUNTING HINT

Rabbits are related to hares. Snowshoe hares have large, furry back feet. This helps them run quickly without sinking into the snow.

There are several kinds of cottontail rabbits found across the United States.

HELPFUL HUNTING

Not all small-game hunting is for sport. Animals such as foxes, groundhogs, and rabbits can be considered vermin. Rabbits and groundhogs destroy crops and fields. Foxes eat chickens. Hunting is often the best way to get rid of these pests.

These animals are usually only considered pests because there are too many of them. They have fewer natural predators—such as wolves and bobcats—in the wild these days. Without predators, vermin populations can grow out of control.

HUNTING HINT

Hunters actually help the **environment** by keeping vermin populations under control.

Foxes live in forests, in meadows, and on farmland across the United States. They're smart and can run very fast—up to 45 miles (72 km) per hour.

A DIFFERENT VIEW

Anti-hunting **activists** are people who don't like the idea of small animals being hunted just for fun. They work hard to make small-game hunting illegal, or against the law. They make a few good points. For example, some hunters are mean and enjoy making animals suffer.

Luckily, most hunters are **humane**. Game laws are in place to keep animals safe, and good hunters obey them. Hunting is about killing an animal quickly and cleanly so it doesn't suffer. Good hunters love the natural world and have respect for the animals they hunt.

GLOSSARY

activist: Someone who acts strongly in support of or against an issue.

bullet: A small object made to be fired from a weapon.

challenge: Something requiring extra effort.

environment: The conditions that surround a living thing and affect the way it lives.

humane: Marked by care for other humans and animals.

instinct: The feeling every creature has that helps it know what to do.

license: An official paper giving someone the right to do something.

pellet: A tiny, round object, often fired from a weapon.

pulley: A wheel or set of wheels used with a rope or chain to lift or lower heavy objects.

target: Something that is aimed at.

vermin: Animals that cause trouble for humans.

INDEX

WEBSITES

Due to the changing nature of Internet links, PowerKids Press has developed
an online list of websites related to the subject of this book. This site is updated
regularly. Please use this link to access the list: www.powerkidslinks.com/hunt/small